SOMETIMES YOU JUST HAVE TO TAKE YOUR WIG OFF AND RUN IN THE RAIN

SOMETIMES YOU JUST HAVE TO TAKE YOUR WIG OFF AND RUN IN THE RAIN

(An honest and humorous step by step journey of a breast cancer survivor)

Beverly B. Still

authorHOUSE®

AuthorHouse™
1663 Liberty Drive
Bloomington, IN 47403
www.authorhouse.com
Phone: 1-800-839-8640

Published by AuthorHouse   05/20/2013

ISBN: 978-1-4817-5550-4 (sc)
ISBN: 978-1-4817-5648-8 (e)

FOREWORD

My name is Beverly B. Still, and I am a breast cancer survivor. It is my hope that this book will help anyone who is facing breast cancer themselves or going through it with a family member or friend. I am taking you step by step through my journey, and I have tried to make it as entertaining as possible.

In order to have a better appreciation for this self-evaluation, you need to know a few things about me personally. I am an English teacher who has been teaching for 28+ years. While I am not a "prima Dona", I am quite a girly girl. I love pretty clothes, and I get my nails done regularly. I love jewelry, sparkly things, and chocolate. I am not a petite lady. I am a plus-sized, tall woman who walks confidently and who is appropriately accessorized when in public. My dark brown/black hair is my crowning glory. I have always had wonderful hair thanks to my parent's genealogy. Oh how I love my makeup, too! I love to play around with all kinds of makeup and never leave home without it.

I enjoy the beach, tanning in the real sun, reading, playing with my dog, and watching fun shows on television. I also like to catch up with my friends and family on the phone or on facebook weekly. I am a very loyal friend and confidant. My husband and I have no children of our own, so I often "adopt" those of my friends for an afternoon or night. My students are my children for the most part . . . but they leave every year and move on to the next chapter in their lives.

I am definitely a people-person. Laughter is a must for every day I am alive. If you can't find humor in life, then I think you aren't really living. Humor is as essential to me as breathing.

I am a teetotaler who has a strong belief in God. I was raised in the church and worked as a pianist and song director in churches when I was in high school and college. I was a music major in college prior to becoming an English major. I give God all the glory for His blessings and strength during my journey.

Table of Contents

Chapter One

February 26th, Lumps in my Mashed Potatoes

It is often said around the South that "God looks after fools and babies." I suppose I fall in the first category even though I am well educated and am presently an English teacher. It is really strange how one who is educated, computer-savvy, and medically responsible could end up with a large breast cancer tumor. You see, I felt this lumpy place at the base of my right breast for around 8 months before deciding to seek a professional opinion. Well, that's not totally true. In late August I called the office where I get my mammograms and asked if I could get one to see what was going on with me. I was told I had to have a referral from a physician to get scanned again before my April appointment. Really??? Like anyone who is sane would ASK for an additional mammogram without a good reason???

So I rationalized. I just knew my bra underwire was aggravating a cyst or something. Then I was convinced my new hyper 85 pound dog had jumped up on me and hit me causing a bruise. Then I was sure I had a stopped up lymph gland. After all, everything I read on the Internet said that painful lumps on the breast were almost always benign.

One sleepless weekend in late February, I had run out of excuses. The lump was getting larger and, as a stomach sleeper, I was not able to rest much since it hurt. I stuffed a pillow underneath me and tried, but I just couldn't get comfortable. That Sunday night I called Janet, who is a science professor with great understanding of the human body. I asked her what she thought about it. Her response was, "Well, you most likely have a stopped up milk gland and will have to get it expirated. It will hurt, but will be over soon. But, you need to go ahead and call your OBGYN and make an appointment and let them check it out." I listened to her, but I still thought, "OBGYN! I have had a complete hysterectomy. I have no need to see that man again!" Nevertheless, the next morning I called.

Chapter Two

February 28th, The Day My World Flipped

I went in to see the nurse practitioner who said, "Yes, I feel what you are talking about. Let's get you scheduled for a mammogram and ultrasound." She called and made an appointment for me the next morning at 9 at my usual place with my favorite tech. I was about 10 weeks early for my annual mammogram, so I thought this would be no big deal at all. I went in like I always do, chipper and ready to get this over and done. I signed in and was called back quickly. Sherry, my favorite tech, was listening to me jabber about the sore place and how I just wanted to get my mind relieved and stop worrying. She did her work quietly. Too quietly. She moved my shoulder-length hair back and said something about my pretty necklace, and I heard a catch in her voice . . . . at least I think I did.

We went back to the ultrasound room then. I watched the screen as the tech moved the wand over the base of my right breast. I saw a dark area, but that was all I noticed. She told me to put back on my top, but not my bra in case we needed to get another shot for the doctor to look at. Within 5 minutes, the doctor, Sherry, the lab tech, and another nurse I didn't know came in the room. The doctor said, "How are you today, Mrs. Still?" I answered, "I'll be just fine when you tell me this is nothing and I can go home." He said, "I'm afraid I can't do that."

My master's degree in English decided to fly out the door at that point as I uttered the lovely syllable, "huh?" He repeated himself, and I sat there for a few seconds and said, "Are you saying I have breast cancer?" He said, "I'm afraid so." My head was spinning, and I felt numb. Then I got a little teary and said, "Sherry, what am I going to do? What do I do?" She hugged me and said, "You're doing it."

My first thought was of the horrible news I had to break to my parents. We are a close-knit family of three . . . I am their only child. In fact, the other day my mother said in her blessing of the food, "Let us draw closer together as a family and closer to You." When it was over, I said, "Mother, the only way we could get closer is if we super-glued ourselves together. And I, for one, don't want to go potty with you unless I am forced to."

So, once I wrapped my head around the fact that I had to face this mountain, my first question to the doctor was, "What is the next step?" He told me that I would need a biopsy done of the tumor. (So that was the identity of the dark spot on ultrasound!) I asked when we could do it, and he told me to reschedule an appointment for it later that week. I then replied, "You found this, now get it out! Can't you biopsy today?" He chuckled and said he could. After it was over, he asked if there was anything else he could do for me, and I responded, "Yeah, get the rest of that tumor out!" He told me I'd probably appreciate some anesthesia before the tumor was removed. Then he asked for a surgeon's name to contact and I was clueless. He began calling out names, and I heard one name I recognized as a friend of a friend. I chose him.

I thought I was finally on the way to escape from that place, but they way-laid me again. I got routed into another office to talk to a nurse whose sister had had a tumor the size of mine and was a survivor. She did ask me if I was taking any type of hormone. I told her I had been taking Premarin pills ever since my hysterectomy. I asked her point blank if I should stop taking them. She nodded yes. She told me most breast cancers are estrogen-fed, and Premarin is estrogen.

Then I had to meet the breast health navigator before I left the office. What the heck is that??? The only thing I wanted to do was sail my tail out of that office; to pinch myself and wake up from this nightmare; to shake my head until things began making sense again . . . . take your pick. But then I met Ellen. I had an appointment to meet with her the day my biopsy came back with the diagnosis of the type of cancer I had. Now to my parent's house.

Chapter Three

February 28th, The Misery Continues

I numbly drove out of the parking lot to my parents' house. They live one block down the road from my house . . . did I mention we were close? I knew my dad was going in to substitute at my high school at 11:30, and it was pushing toward 11, so I hurried there before he left. I walked in as usual and the two of them were standing in the hallway talking and wondering what was taking me so long. They said, "How'd it go?" I replied, "Not the way I expected." I gave them a minute to absorb that one. Then I said, "They told me I have breast cancer." My mom grabbed the door facing, and my dad turned pale as a ghost. I said, "Don't worry. Things are not like they used to be. I'll just probably go through 6 months of hell and then be fine. There's no need to worry until we know facts." Yeah, it sounded lame to me too. I knew they didn't buy it, but it was the best sales pitch I could come up with at the moment.

Dad had to go. He was still pale, and he said, "You ARE going to stay with your mother until I get home, aren't you?" I told him I would. Mother and I went to her bed and just sat and lay there talking about what would most likely be happening. I recounted the whole scenario for her and she just nodded. She didn't cry. After about an hour she just HAD to go to Walgreens to get a couple of items. I knew what she was doing. She was going to call her good friend, Jane Brown, whom we all suspect has a hotline straight to God.

Well, I wasn't wrong. She returned in 30-45 minutes with red eyes and sniffles. I said, "You called Jane, didn't you?" She nodded. I told her it was going to be fine. She said that she felt better and had turned it over to God. I was relieved. Little did I know at the time, but Dad was over at the high school losing it. He told Mrs. Brookins, an assistant principal, about my diagnosis and began crying. Well, that drew a crowd. My dad is not a small-size person, and he definitely does not cry in public. So much for discretion at my workplace! Oh well, I probably would have told it anyway.

Chapter Four

February 29th, Yes, It was a Leap Year

I went to work that Tuesday and told my students. I had three classes of general seniors and three classes of honors sophomores. They were equally speechless. I got hugs and tears . . . . some were sincere and others were typical teens who just love drama. For the most part, they were all really sweet and supportive. I told them I would keep them posted about it all and I would be in school as much as possible. The next day would be biopsy results day, so I had to be home.

March 1

I received the call from my OBGYN around 10 the next morning. He was trying to gently tell me I had cancer, and I told him I already knew that. He then told me I had a 5.1 tumor that was classified as invasive ductal carcinoma. It meant that my cancer began in the milk duct and had grown outside of the duct. He said we would do a scan to see if it was to or through the chest wall. I was scheduled to scan the next day. Meanwhile, I was set up to see the surgeon on Friday, but he cancelled because he would not have the scan results until Monday.

Now to go meet with this breast navigator chick named Ellen. I went to see her around 11:00. I had not been eating very much due to my nerves, but this morning I had two small blueberry muffins and a Coke for breakfast on the way over to see Ellen. I went in to meet with her, and I was comforted and appalled during the same visit. First, she was a sweet, compassionate, and understanding person to talk to. She asked me if I had questions, and I said, "Tell me everything."

Ellen patiently explained the various treatments and surgery options for my type of tumor; which, by the way, was 98% estrogen-fed. She said that my surgeon and I would make those decisions together. She told me that she had a tumor basically the same size as mine and was 4 years cancer-free. We discussed surgery, recovery time, and prognoses. Then Ellen got into her research on nutrition and the effects of foods on cancer. She told me that sugar FED cancer. I replied, "Then my cancer is deliriously happy." She asked what I had for breakfast and I told her. Another sad shake of the head. I looked longingly out of her office window at the Sonic across the street as she talked about only eating organic foods and filtered waters and green teas. I finally said, "So there's nothing I can drive through and eat?" She replied not really, and I went into depression. I don't cook. It's not that I can't cook, but I don't. Insert long story about husband who didn't clean up after I cooked at this point.

On I go tell my mother all the info that Ellen shared. I give her the multi-page copy of what's good and what's bad to eat. BIG MISTAKE. HUGE. I was basically on a starvation diet for the next month. In fact, the biggest melt-down I had throughout this ordeal was the night she promised me an egg-custard and I got one made with Stevia and no crust. But, I am getting ahead of myself.

Mom and I went to Publix to purchase allowed foods. We each spent around $200.00 for organic eggs, chicken, and cheese, organic cabbage, carrots, and whole wheat pasta. We bought whole grain brown bread, Stevia, molasses, berries, and Brita water pitchers. We bought yogurt and, thankfully, I picked up some Cinnamon Life cereal. I think the dry cereal kept me from starvation on more than one occasion. I was definitely eating healthier, and I didn't enjoy it one minute.

Chapter Five

March 6th, Meet the Surgeon

I met Dr. Johns and listened to him explain my options for treatment. My response was, "Please get this out of me—now. Take it all. Take them both. Get the lymph nodes. Just get it all out." He smiled. He said that was an aggressive approach. I agreed and said, but is it wrong? He said at my young age he completely agreed with me. Take no chances. I then asked him how long I would have to be out of work. He said usually 4-6 weeks. I argued. I told him that I teach. I need only my eyes, ears, fingers, and mouth to work. He then said maybe 3 weeks out of work if all goes well. The good news was that the cancer had not invaded my chest wall. Thank you Jesus!

We discussed surgery days and Dr. Johns told me he operated on Tuesdays and Thursdays. He had an opening for the next day. I got big eyes, and said, "Could we schedule it for Thursday so I can see my students and get my class ready for my absence?" We agreed. Surgery scheduled for March 8th. Double mastectomy: right side radical. Dannnnnng!

Mother was with me for the entire meeting, so I didn't have to relay any of that info to her. I told my husband what was going to go down, and he said to me, "How are you handling this so calmly? I'd be falling apart." Well, thanks for the positive support there, Skippy. There's an old southern saying about teats on a boar hog that I find applicable here. ☺

Wednesday, March 7

I went to school to tell my students what was about to happen. I prepared them for 2 weeks of classes with my dad as their substitute. Now, this situation is a novel all its own. Some of my students love my dad. Others can't tolerate him because he doesn't tolerate nonsense. Either way, they know I will find out what happens in my classroom when he's there. It relieves a lot of stress for me because I know he knows procedures, how I do things, and he knows my students.

When I went home, I had to pack for the hospital and my parent's house. I had to go to my parent's house because I have Jaxon, the 85 pound golden who thinks he is still little and shows his love by jumping up on you. Did I mention that Jaxon is obsessed with balls? I didn't think the drainage bulbs that I would have attached to me after surgery would be very safe around Jaxon.

My parents insisted I go home with them. I didn't argue except for the fact that I love my bed. That pillow-top mattress with my high thread count sheets is one of my favorite things in the whole wide world. The guest bed at my mom and dad's is horrible. It is too short for long legs and when you move you get really sea-sick. The mattress bounces better than any trampoline you've ever been on.

Super-Dad to the rescue. He says that they will buy a new mattress and he will build a platform to put the mattress on. He tells Steve (the hubs) to measure the height of my box spring and says he's got it covered. He goes to his wood shop and gets busy. I think that was part of the reason he wanted to build this . . . . he wanted to stay busy. We will revisit this a little later. Plans are made. I will be in the hospital for one night and then will go to my parent's house for recovery.

Chapter Six

Ð-Ðay: To Surgery and Beyond

I had to be at the hospital by 6 for an 8 o'clock surgery. We all caravan to the hospital and things move quickly. Unexpectedly fast. I like this hospital. They get things done in a timely manner. It all happened so quickly that I didn't even have time to go to the restroom and worried as I was going under the anesthesia that I might wet myself during surgery. (The weird way the mind works at times is amusing.)

I awoke to the nurses telling me it was all over, and they were moving me to a room. I think I remember hearing the wheels thunking down the hall . . . . but don't hold me to it. The door opened and there were my parents, the hubs, and my aunt and cousin. I did my quick head count, discontinued logical thought and went back to la-la land. When I came to again, the nurses were poking and prodding around. You know blood pressure check, leg compression check, etc. I remember asking the nurse what that large thing was poking out on my chest and she giggled and replied, your breastbone. Huh. Never knew I had a breastbone that large. Oh wait a minute . . . . I was caved in (or carved out) on both sides! And I had three fist-sized ticks attached to my body. I named them Huey, Dewey, and Louie. They were my drainage bulbs and would stick with me for a few weeks.

The next coherent moment I saw my pretty flowers and presently declared that I was hot. I was on the 4th floor of the hospital, and you know hot air rises. Even in early March, heat can be a factor in lower Alabama. A sweet nurse found me an oscillating pedestal fan, and I could've hugged her. The next time I saw her she was leaving from her shift and brought in the night nurse to introduce us . . . . only I knew that face. It was the face of one of my former students. Instant humiliation! No makeup, plastered hair, tubes and bulbs hanging all over me, all my personal business in my file . . . shall I go on? Oh well. I was glad he and I got along well, and he harbored nothing but good will toward me. Otherwise, I would have made a run for it . . . . okay a spirited shuffle for it.

Late that afternoon after surgery, I had a visit from my navigator friend, Ellen. She brought me a cute little butterfly pillow, card, and other goodies and talked to me about what I should expect next. She also brought materials for me to read through. I asked her how she was doing because she seemed a little disconcerted. She smiled sadly and told me her sister had just been diagnosed with breast cancer too. Wow. This "invisible worm that flies in the night" is making its way around south Alabama.

Early evening I had a visit from Jane who proclaimed that my color was already looking better. Around 10 my friend, May, came by to check up on me before she went home for the night. Mother came to stay with me, although I told her not to. Believe it or not, we slept soundly.

The next morning, I am ready to get the doo-dah out of dodge. Dr. Johns comes by and tells me everything went great. He's sure he got the entire tumor removed. He also tells me he removed 24 lymph nodes from the right side and we will hear the pathology report from them by next week. After that visit, I am instructed by the nurses how to drain the bulbs and measure the contents and record them on the spreadsheet they provided. I glanced at mom and said, "This looks like your job." I got a pain pill for the road, and then we were going to be dismissed. Only they forgot to take out the IV needle from my left hand . . . so I did it. Did I mention I was ready to go home?

Arrival at mom and dad's house was fine, but I was really tired. I sat at the table, drank some iced tea, and was ready to try out the new bed. I was not prepared for what I saw when I walked into the room. Have you ever seen the Carol Burnett version of "The Princess and the Pea" with the stacks and stacks of mattresses up to the ceiling? Well, there was only one stack and one mattress . . . . but that was one heck of a climb up. I had to have a stepping stool to get up there. The ceiling fan was a little too close for comfort. If I hadn't been unable to move around much, I would have freaked a little. Needless to say, an error in measuring had been made. Had my nose been longer, it would have been in danger of getting shortened with each pass of the fan blade.

Friday, Saturday, and Sunday were basically a blur. I slept, drank water, got sponge baths, emptied drainage bulbs, and took pain pills. Each day I got a little stronger. Finally by Monday I was ready to join the world somewhat.

I wanted a shower!!! Badly! Dad found a shower chair and put it in my shower. Mom got soaked helping me shower, but it felt so wonderful. She changed my bandages over the drainage bulbs and I put on clean pj's and got clean sheets on the bed. I was beginning to feel alive. It was a little disconcerting to walk by the mirror, however. My stomach looked like I was 6 months pregnant because I had no boobage to balance out my torso. I then began to wonder how I would ever leave the house in this condition.

Mom said she would call Ellen, the navigator, and ask what there was to help fill out my shirt after surgery. Ellen gave Mom a number for a lady in Ashford to assist with this dilemma. I got an appointment for Thursday. Slowly I was beginning to get ready to join the world again.

Chapter Seven

All the King's Horses and All the King's Men Tried to Put Beverly Together Again.

During the first three days after surgery, life was simple and I was groggy from the pain pills. After that, I began getting really hungry and wanted real food. My mom didn't let me have anything to eat other than approved foods from the Ellen list. I could have yogurt, eggs, or berries for breakfast. For lunch I had a whole wheat sandwich with organic chicken or turkey. For dinner I had whole wheat pasta with a little tomato sauce, salsa, and chunks of chicken. I even got a little cheese on top—organic of course. It was during these days that I began to get quite grumpy from my limited food choices. I was losing weight, but that was not my goal for the moment.

On Wednesday, I saw the surgeon and found out that NOT ONE of the 24 lymph nodes tested positive for cancer. Praise God!! I really expected at least a few of them to be positive. I wouldn't let myself dream that they would all be clear. I guess this is a mark against my faith because "our Jane" had prayed for me and anointed me prior to surgery. I have never had this done before. It was really sweet and sobering. Jane claimed God's promises that He would hear us and heal us. I told you she had a direct line to God!

Dr. Johns checked the stitches, the drains, and said everything looked great. He then said that he would dismiss me once the drains came out. He discussed chemotherapy and asked me to think about it seriously because it was poison. Why would I poison my body to lower my chances of recurrence from 20 to 10 percent? It made sense to me. I took him at his word, and in my mind chemo was not even an option. I was a happy girl!

The next day Steve drove me to Ashford and I met a sweet lady named Patricia. She took me into her private office and talked to me about the options I had for things to help me look a little more normal . . . even with the drains still in. As she talked, she told me that she was going through chemo herself for breast cancer. I confidently told her I was not going to have to get chemo and she said I was very very lucky. It was then I noticed her eyes looked weak and she had no eyelashes. Patricia patiently found a white cotton undershirt type garment that had Velcro closings and puffy white pads to put in for boobage. There was even a little place on both sides for the drain bulbs. Cool stuff!! I walked out of the place looking a whole lot better than I had going in. My anatomy was looking more like it should, and I had made a good friend in the process.

With my new "girls" underneath my clothes, I was ready to go in public for a change of scenery. I think we went to Cracker Barrel for supper that night. It was yummy, and I felt like I was joining the human race again just one full week after surgery. I'm not going to tell you that I was full of energy and jumping around. I had to gauge my activities and rest in-between my visits or outings. In another week, I was much better. Still sore, still having to deal with the bulbs and drainage, but better. I had found a way to sleep kind of on my side rather than having to face the ceiling. It was great! I couldn't wait until I could flip all the way over on my stomach to sleep.

Chapter Eight

Week Two at Mom's and I Miss My Dog!

I have been at mom and dad's house for over a week, and I am getting tired of not having a television in the bedroom and sleeping on the ceiling. I convinced my dad to let me buy the box springs for the mattress to get back to a normal sleeping height. I was able to turn now, and I didn't want to have a brush with the ceiling fan or fall to my death. So, dad gets Steve to help him out with transporting and buying the box springs. Steve wanted to buy 2 box springs from Sam's. No one knows why, but that's just Steve. He does provide entertainment!

The big wooden box is disassembled and moved out. Box springs are brought in. Mattress is no longer up in the stratosphere. Hallelujah! I miss my sloppy kisses from my golden retriever. I know he's rough. He is like lightening. He thinks he is still a tiny puppy. But he's my baby. Super Dad says that he thinks he has thought of a way to let me visit with him briefly. I'm listening. I turn a dining room chair backward with a big pillow between my body and the chair back. We pull up two more chairs. One in front of me with the seat facing out, and the other chair is blocking my side from Jaxon's hyper self. Steve brings my baby in mom's house on a leash, and he is glad to see me. Not exuberant. I think he was a little "pistocated" with me for leaving him for so long. He didn't hurt me at all. It was nice to see him even though I got somewhat of a cold shoulder.

My mom and dad's dog, Maxx, was gentler and kinder and older. So, I had to make do with his kisses for a few more days. Did I mention that Maxx is a black lab that weighs 143 pounds? Yep. He looks more like a black stallion than a lab.

I get lots of company at this point. Former students, current senior students (Anna and Tiffany who were my aides and in SGA), and some of mom and dad's Sunday school class members came by to see me. I got so many restaurant gift cards from my co-workers and various other friends and neighbors; it was overwhelming. See, they ALL know I don't cook anymore!! My cousin, Yvonne, called me every day to check on how I was doing. My dad kept me informed about my students and their antics. Time clicked on. I was hungry. I had begun putting Cinnamon Life cereal in a plastic container by my bed at night so when I woke up to my stomach growling, I could silence it.

I told my mom I needed something GOOD to eat. She had been so sweet about cooking just the right stuff, but I was getting better and wanted some real food. She told me she would fix me an egg custard that night. I went in for my afternoon nap dreaming of it. I LOVE egg custard. I went in to supper and sat down. I ate my meal and saved room for the dessert. I watched in horror as mother brought out a glass dish of custard (no crust) with the wrong consistency. I looked at her as if she was the biggest traitor in the entire country. I asked, "Did you make that with sweetener and not sugar?" She nodded yes, and I swear I teared up. I had been teased with promises of one of my favorite foods and in its place was a tasteless Xerox copy of what I wanted. I think I stormed out of the kitchen and went to my room to pout. I really don't want to remind you that I am a grown woman. I acted like a complete child . . . . and I knew it. I just couldn't control myself. As my cousin would say, I had a "come apart." My poor mom. She had been cooking and trying so hard and here I am acting like a buffoon.

Once I had remembered my age and my manners again, I explained to mother that I wanted something real and sweet. We remembered the ice cream sandwiches in her freezer, and she and I began inhaling 1 and a half each. I was all better at that point.

At my weekly appointment with the surgeon, he removed two of my drains (Huey and Dewey). That left me with only one "tick."

Louie had to stick around for another week. Dang it. I was tired of him hanging around getting my blood.

My parents had been great, wonderful, and all the other adjectives that mean stupendous. But I wanted to go home now. I had stayed an extra weekend over the two weeks with them, but I was ready for my room, my computer, my television, my air conditioner, my food, and my dog. Steve would be there too. He was helpful for picking up food for supper . . . . especially if we used those gift cards.

Mom and Dad did everything they could to try to keep me there, but I was determined. Louie and I went home. Jaxon was so happy to see me back. He did jump on me when I was sitting in the recliner, but it wasn't a disaster. I had to act fast, but no harm; no foul. Things are getting better all the time. Spring is in the air and I would have returned to school to teach, but Graduation exams are going on and classes are not even close to normal. Dad has it all together, and I decide to go back the week after spring break—which was the following week.

At the third office visit with Dr. Johns, I finally lose Louie. He dismisses me and sets up an appointment with the oncologist, Dr. Sullivan just to verify that I didn't need chemo. I go home and read in the sun on my kindle. The birds are singing and I'm feeling better and better. I make another trip to see my Ashford friend, Patricia for my stage two boobs. She tells me that I can't wear them until I am completely healed up from the drains. So, I am hoping I can wear them when I return to school again. The first stage cotton puffs have a bad habit of migrating north, and when you have no feeling in your chest, before you realize it you have boobs under your chin. Literally.

My cousin and I made a day trip to the beach during spring break. She laughed at me so much. Remember, all I had at this point were the light-weight cotton puff boobs. I put them in my bathing suit top and it looked fine when I was standing up. It was when I lay down on the beach that "things fell apart." I was flashing snow-white puffs on all sides when laying out. I finally said to Yvonne, "Shut up laughing. Would you rather see me concave, or with my white puffs showing?" We agreed the white was a better option; so, modesty and decorum out the window once again. A few months ago I would have just died of embarrassment to be in public like that. Now I am happy to be at the beach in the sun with no worries. My appointment at the oncologist is in 2 days. Things will change again.

Chapter Nine

No Chemo for Me . . . . What?

Well, here I go off to another doctor's office to meet with yet another doctor. I have no dread at all because I know from what Dr. Johns said that I have nothing to worry about. It was then that I met Carrie, Dr. Sullivan's nurse practitioner. She is this little petite cheerleader-looking Barbie doll with a bubbly personality. Such a sweet Southern belle. We got along famously. I cracked jokes, and she laughed. That was, until. Until she said the words, "Well you had a huge tumor." I replied, "5.1?" She said, "No, honey. Yours was a 6.3." I looked quite confused and she said, "They forgot to add back in the size of the biopsy. It was 1.2, so total you had a 6.3. We always do chemo for anything over a 5."

Suddenly Barbie wasn't looking so cute. I asked her the one thing I didn't want to know. "Am I going to lose my hair?" She nodded yes. I had not cried at all during all of this. I had come close twice, but no real tears. Make that three close calls now. I just did suck it up in time. She then said, "You may lose your eyelashes and eyebrows too, but they'll grow back. Look at the bright side. You won't have to worry about shaving your legs all summer!"

Then she sets up all kinds of body scans for me to be sure nothing is wrong with any other organs, tissue, or bones. She also sets up a test to see what type of tumor I had . . . the oncotype. I asked what that was. She said that test tells if the tumor has a high rate of recurrence. We will know more how to get the right dosage of chemo based on that information.

Well, chin on the ground, I get back in my car and go home to digest this latest information. It is giving me heartburn. Oh, the hospital was really quick about scheduling the body scans. I had a call that afternoon for the following day. I was going to get both done on the same day. Yippee.

I show up for tests and have to drink this horrible "flavored water". I had the choice of lemon or berry. I picked lemon. DON'T pick the lemon. I had to return one lemon for a berry in order to get it all down. Yuk. This nice young Asian man took me in for the organ scan and told me he would leave the room for me to undress from the top only. I told him, "Just give me a minute and I'll be one of the boys." He blushed so red that I had to giggle. I didn't mean to crush his professional composure, but I guess I did. I had to hold my breath to keep from laughing the entire time. His expression was priceless.

I had to return in an hour and a half for the bone part of the test. The lady who was doing this test said, "Our tech forgot to get you to sign this form this morning. I'm going to have to get him! I laughed and said, 'It was my fault.'" I then recounted what had happened and she laughed so hard I thought she needed oxygen. Yep; yep; you know me. I'm the crazy woman from the big cit-ty.

The bone scan was fine until they got to my feet. She scanned and rescanned. I had to move my feet to another position and she scanned again. I finally asked, "What are you looking at on my feet?" Another tech said, "Do you have some old trauma on your feet?" I said, "Absolutely. Why didn't she ask me?" You see, I fell off a cliff (about 18') when I was 12 years old at a Bible camp when my moccasin shoes hit thick pine straw. I tried to fly, but my wings didn't work. I hit the pavement below on my feet; bounced; hit on my knees; bounced; and hit on my boo-tay and stayed put. The tech nodded and said, "Yep. That would explain it."

Okay. I have been scanned. Waiting to hear from Onco and then schedule the beginning of chemo. I met with Barbie Sunshine once again and found that Onco was not my friend. I had a high risk of recurrence. I was going to get a full dosage of chemo, and I couldn't get in the sun all summer until chemo was over. Whoo-hoo. Meanwhile I had met back with Patricia in Ashford and found that she was beginning round two of chemo on the same day I was going for the first time. Also, Ellen had been keeping in touch with me and she planned to come bring me some crushed ice during my first visit. Ellen had told me that she played softball after getting her chemo, so I wasn't really concerned about having bad reactions. Ellen was about the same size as Carrie. I knew that I had lots more of me to dilute the chemo, so problemo. Time to buy a wig.

I took one of my adopted students, Tiffany, with me wig shopping. It was difficult. I thought I would have lots of choices, but that was not the case. You have to try them all on, because you cannot tell anything about how they will look on your head from the mannequins. We finally found a few that would "do" and narrowed it down to one or two. Tiffany kept me giggling with her wig antics. She kept plopping colorful wigs on top of her long black hair. It was too funny! I got my cousin and mother to meet me at the wig shop the next day for a second opinion. We all agreed on one and I bought it. Good wigs are NOT cheap. I took it to my hairdresser and she cut it to look like my normal hair. I think I'm ready.

Chapter Ten

Chemo Begins

May third was the first day of chemo. I went in, a little nervous. How do I know? I think I went to the restroom about 5 times during the two hours I was there. Ridiculous! I got the combo of Cytoxin and Taxotere, with the Neulasta shot the next day. I was told the shot caused more reaction than the chemo. I was fine that Thursday with the exception of my taste. From the moment the first chemo hit my bloodstream my taste changed. I was fine Friday. Saturday I began running a low fever and felt like I had a light case of the flu. My leg bones ached, and sharp pains in them made me groan and flinch. I stayed in bed Saturday, Sunday, and Monday.

I returned to work on Tuesday, but was feeling rough. Wednesday and Thursday were fine. I got up on Friday and I looked like I had boiling hot water poured all over my right side from the shoulder down to my waist. One part looked red and angry. The other part looked like I had been fried in a tanning bed. I was a hot mess. I called the doctor's office and asked to see someone. The head nurse, Lana, said she would just call in a prescription for me. I insisted that she needed to see what was happening. She reluctantly agreed and I went in to the office at 1. When I saw her at 2, she was dumbstruck upon seeing my skin. She asked me if I had had radiation. I told her no, I had just begun chemo. She gave me two prescriptions and told me that they would see me in 2 weeks for another dose. I told her I did not want another Neulasta shot . . . ever. A month or so later, Lana told me that she had thought I was a hypochondriac until she saw my reaction. Then she said I had the worst reaction she had ever seen.

After the first chemo dose, I was told I had 14 days before my hair began to fall out. Well, being the hard-headed take-charge person I am, I decided to get my shoulder-length hair chopped off. Short. For once I told my hairdresser to do whatever she wanted to do, and make it short. She did. I know I lost at least 3 pounds of hair that afternoon. Marsha (my hairdresser) was so sweet. She praised me for taking charge and said I was doing the right thing. She also wouldn't accept any money for the haircut. She said it was the least she could do for me.

When I returned to school with my microscopic new doo, my colleagues and friends loved it. Even the students said they liked it. After a few days, I began to believe people were actually being sincere. Two of my close friends, Jim and Jennifer, told me I looked at least 10 years younger. Well, if that's true, I need to go wig shopping again. I guess I need a short wig. I ordered one and hoped it would be here before the great fall-out occurred.

Fourteen days after chemo exactly my hair began letting go. I ran my fingers through the top of my hair and wads would be in my fingers. I didn't like this at all. I went down the street to mom's and asked dad to give me a GI haircut. He didn't believe me for a moment, but then he saw I was serious. He got his razor and began the process. I sat on the patio in the swing and he began buzzing. Maxx the doggie-horse was quite confused as my hair began falling to the floor. Mom watched, shaking her head in disbelief. I laughed at the new weird feeling of my head. It was a lot cooler now! And I looked like a cue ball with make up on. My head was so WHITE. Strange. I told Daddy that I was only one step short of being the boy he always wanted . . . . but not to get his hopes up for that last stage. We laughed.

The short wig made it in. Some of my students didn't even know when I began wearing the wig. Victory!! Be sure to celebrate all the small victories on this journey.

Chapter Eleven

Chemo Treatment Part Deux

I returned to the oncology office on May 24th for chemo dose #2. Dr. Sullivan met with me and said that due to my severe reaction they were changing my Taxotere to the newer and improved drug, Abraxane. I would not have to take the Neulasta shot again. (That was good because I was planning to say no.) The catch was that I would have to come in every week for the Abraxane. And every third week I would get a dose of Cytoxin too. Well, it was almost summer, so the every week deal would not be a problem. Dr. Sullivan seemed excited about the whole change, so I was cool with it.

Let me tell you about Dr. Sullivan's set up. It's pretty sweet. In his office there are private rooms with the reclining chairs so patients can nap if they choose to do so. There are television sets hooked up to cable with VCR players and movies, and there are magazines. If you have to go through this process, the set up is really nice. Once I was put in the common room—where chairs are lined up like old beauty shop dryers and everyone can watch everyone else. I learned to count my blessings that day. It kind of gives you a big stab in the heart to see the little frail, tiny old people having to get chemo. In fact, if you want or need a lesson in humility, just visit an oncology office. It will break your heart.

So May 24th I get Abraxane and Cytoxin. No major problems other than loss of taste, appetite, and fatigue. No nausea. I was lucky. I go get my treatments June 7 and 14. I had begun to have many problems physically at this point. I had stomach aches, diarrhea, yeast infections, extreme fatigue, loss of appetite, and really felt like warmed over poo.

When my mom and I left Dr. Sullivan's office on the 14th, we walked out to a downpour. I don't mean a strong shower. I mean a deluge. The parking lot looked like a waterway. The sky was deep blue-gray and there was no sign of it letting up. My mom is in her mid-70's and not real surefooted for several physical reasons. She and I looked at each other and she told me she would go out and get the car. I told her no, I knew what to do. I instructed her to stay under the shelter with the rest of the crowd who were also trying to figure out how to leave the hospital. I carried a big purse, so I jerked off my wig, put it in my purse, and walked out (bald as a goose) to my car in the hard rain. I was soaked because I couldn't run or even walk quickly, but I made it into my car. I picked my mom up with my bald head still dripping and shining for all the crowd to see. She began fussing at me and I said, "Mother, sometimes you've just got to take your wig off and run in the rain." My pride was gone, but my determination was strong. Whatever it takes, I'm not going to let this get the best me.

One of my worst days was June 18th. That Monday I went to school to tutor kids for the graduation exam as I had promised to do for the summer session. The air conditioning was off in the building. It was hotttt weather, and I had no energy. I felt like my body and my legs had divorced each other. By the time I got a room to teach in, I was about to fall out. I was sweating profusely, I felt sick, and I couldn't think straight. I made it to noon, but I was totally wiped out. My legs felt like the bones inside had turned to jelly. By the time I wobbled to my car and cooled off, I was spent. I wasn't able to teach the next day. I was still recovering. I managed to make it all the other days for 2 ½ to 3 hours rather than the 4 I could have worked. That Thursday the 21st I went to Dr. Sullivan's office with a laundry list of everything that was "torn up" in my body. My counts were low, so I got a smaller dose and two weeks off.

I was so excited to get two weeks off. Just as I began to feel human (the last three days of my fourteen off), it was time to go get dosed again. I got the Abraxane on July 12th, then the Cytoxin on July 19th. My fingers and my toes began to be numb. The sharp pains in my legs continued. Even my bed was tired of me. I didn't want anything much to eat. I would just nibble on fresh fruit, blueberry muffins, Nilla wafers, cheese crackers, lemonade, and chicken dumplings or noodles. I had long since forgotten the forbidden foods list. I just had to eat to survive at this point.

I need to tell you that the night after an afternoon treatment was horribly inconvenient. I don't know what made my kidneys kick into overdrive, but I got very little sleep every time after getting my IV drugs. Even my baby-dog Jaxon was disgusted at having his sleep disrupted so many times. I felt sorry for him and his sad eyes for about a minute. Then I remembered his high energy level and told him to just deal with it . . . because I had to.

Dr. Sullivan told me that the numbness was a side effect of the Abraxane and it could be permanent. I began taking another prescription for neuropathy. The numbness began creeping higher. My legs were numb from the knee down and my arms numb from the elbows down. Walking began to be difficult. I walked like an 80 year old woman. Great. It's almost time for me to begin teaching again and I'm hairless, have no eyelashes or eyebrow on the right side, and now I walk like a little old granny. This too shall pass . . . . but when?

I went in to one visit with Dr. Sullivan to tell him I was not going to do this anymore. My body was poisoned, and I was ready to get better. He listened. Then he told me, "I have ONE chance to make you a survivor, and this is it. If you stop now, your chances are not great. If you finish you have a much better chance of being a survivor." Well, what could I say to that? Basically, nothing. I had to suck it up and finish this.

Chapter Twelve

The End of Chemo is in Sight and Radiation is Coming Up Next

School began on August 20th and I still had 4 treatments left. I am very honest with my students, and wondered how I would tell them about what was going on with me at this point. I could just picture one of them knocking me or shoving me accidently and my wig flying off. I didn't want them to go into total shock. I already had the dogs quite confused, no need to torture the kids too. One of my opening day activities has always been "Take Your Best Guess about Your Teacher." This is where I list 20-25 "facts" about me, and have them guess which ones are true and which are false. This year I put as one of my "facts", I am bald as a goose. They all looked at me and giggled as they wrote false. Then I had my chance to tell them about my summer and how I only lacked 4 more treatments. They were all so sweet. (I have all sophomores this year.)

When I returned from my last treatment, the classes clapped. They celebrated with me. It was heartwarming. I then began radiation during fall break and finished up during Christmas break.

I loved my radiologist too. I have had great doctors and nurses to this point. Dr. Raj was my radiologist. He was definitely from an Indian ancestry, but when he opened his mouth and spoke in a distinctly Southern accent, I almost fell out of my chair. It took me a minute to wrap my brain around that one. He told me he was born and raised in Alabama . . . . and I believed him.

Well, my body said it was going to rebel again. With just two weeks of treatments behind me, I developed radiation acne. The best way I can describe it is to compare it to sun poisoning. It was red, itchy, bumpy, and then it was dry. I had to get another prescription for that. Had I known what was ahead of me on this journey, I would have taken out stock in Walgreens first! Due to my students sharing their various bugs like virus and flu, I got behind on my treatments. On New Year's Eve I took my last one. My underarm on the right side looks like I smeared black shoe polish on my skin. My right chest looks quite tan . . . the left quite pale. But I finished. I finished. I've finished chemo, and I've finished radiation. Please, God, let me honestly say I have finished.

Chapter Thirteen

Objects in Sleeve May Appear Larger Than They Actually Are . . . Or Not

Sometime in mid May my right arm began to enlarge. Really enlarge. I had developed lymphedema. (Remember that I had 24 lymph ducts removed during surgery.) When I saw Dr. Sullivan in June, he scheduled me to get a custom compression sleeve and glove. When I met with Beth, the lymphedema specialist, she told me that I would wear this sleeve and glove every day with the exception of sleeping. I could take it off at night, but that was all. She also told me that she could help me shrink the arm back down to a more normal size with therapy, but I couldn't get the therapy until I had finished radiation.

Just before I finished radiation, I was pulling on my sleeve and my fingernail popped right through it. Uh oh. Now the already picked and pilled old sleeve had a nice run and hole. I called Beth and she said to keep using it because it was almost time to see her for my treatment. I can't tell you how wonderful this news was. It is difficult to dress when one arm is more like another leg than an arm. Blouses fit one-sided with one sleeve so tight it looks awful.

When the sleeve and glove are off, my swollen arm skin is dimpled (the medical term is pitted) from the warped condition it is in. I am about "toe-up from the flow-up." But it is going to get better.

If I thought my clothing fit lop-sided before, when I began therapy and got the serious wraps, it was absolutely ludicrous. Beth did her re-route massage to show my fluids the way out. I had my doubts about this. Then she wrapped my hand and arm. She wrapped and wrapped and wrapped . . . . every finger and my hand with stretchy gauze and a glove; my hand to mid arm with small size elastic bandage; my mid arm to elbow with middle size elastic bandage; my upper arm with large size elastic bandage. Each bandage taped down and then a layer of cotton bandaging on top of that with a stretchy sleeve on top. I looked like my right arm was literally mummified. By now, I could really care less how I looked. The problem was that I am right-handed. When you can't move your arm and can barely move your fingers, you make unpleasant discoveries. I discovered that I had to learn to put on make-up left handed. I had to brush teeth left handed. I had to perform "tolietries" left handed. I had lots of trouble typing too. Horribly inconvenient, but eventually effective.

Chapter Fourteen

Walk On

My journey is not done yet, but I am hoping that I have learned humility. I have learned that I can walk out to my car without boobage, makeup, or hair to go to my mom and dad's. I can wear clothing that doesn't fit properly on one side in public. I can walk better each day. I am stronger every day. I am more appreciative of things now. I will be able to bask in the sunshine this spring and summer. I will get reconstructive surgery this summer so prosthesis won't be necessary any more. My hair is growing . . . slowly. My eyelashes are back. My eyebrow is back. My fingers and toes are still numb, but they are getting better.

Just today I went by to let Marsha, my hairdresser, see the funny hair growing back on my head. It is a different color and texture, but it is hair. She laughed with me at the texture. It feels like a stuffed animal. We discussed the fact that the color is a damaged color and mine will eventually grow back in. She also couldn't resist combing through and trimming it. Yes, trimming my two inch hair. Like I said, celebrate the small things.

I can actually walk all over Sam's Club now. I can type better and better each day. My tummy is not nearly as temperamental, and I don't have sleepless nights of continual toilet trips. I can sleep on my stomach again. I feel like talking to people on the phone and on facebook. I really enjoy teaching and talking to my students again.

On January 15th I met back with Carrie to get started on the "pill" for breast cancer patients. She told me that it was a hormone blocker. Did you know that your muscles produce hormones too? That was news to me! Anyway, after discussing possible side effects, the prescription was written. Here I go toward the next step. Carrie also said that I would need to get bloodline markers and another body scan to be sure everything was as it should be. I set it up for the next school holiday, MLK day.

I remembered the lemon water and made a mental note to get berry for sure this time. But, the biggest difference was my level of nervousness. From that Tuesday through the next Tuesday (when I could call Carrie for results), I began to get progressively more antsy. All of my bravado went out the window. I felt like if I was told I had to go back on chemo at this point that I would just feel like quitting. I've just gotten my hair growing and I am beginning to feel some energy that I have been missing for a very long time.

So, to scan I go. Berry water still tasted like crap, but I managed to get most of the two bottles down. My knees were almost knocking. I felt like an idiot. Scan was over and of course I had to give it a shot. "Can you tell me anything?" I got a negative nod and then was told, "The radiologist has to get paid too, so I can't tell you anything." Dang. I went home and then on to lymphedema therapy. I watched television and read that night prior to going to bed, but I thought I'd never fall asleep. The mind was racing. Tomorrow would be a big day.

Tuesday came and I went to work with my little angels and my little devils. I knew I couldn't call until after lunch, so to say I was a little preoccupied would be an understatement. I called the receptionist after noon and gave the number I could be reached at. The clock ticked. The phone finally rang, and sure enough it was Carrie. My stomach was in knots. She said, "How are you doing today?" I said I was as nervous as a long-tailed cat in a room full of rocking chairs. She laughed. The scan was fine. There was some damage to my right lung from the radiation, but otherwise all was well. My blood marker was also good. It was an eleven. Anything over 32 is cause for concern. I breathed once again. Then I got in the most chipper mood. Relief. Gratefulness. Peace. Joy. Thank you, God.

Throughout this journey there have been so many moments that have been funny, touching, and inspiring. Funny things like the day a new student entered my classroom and saw me wearing a hat and asked, "Is it hat day today?" Funny things like my friend's 3 year old twin boys looking down my shirt at my strange "girls" and asking, "What is THAT?" Funny things like the special education students coming around classrooms for Mardi Gras week giving us beads and my students saying they would rather get theirs the other way, to which one student remarked, "Mrs. Still would sure be out of luck then." ☺

Touching moments like the day one of my students brought me a Survivor pin in October. Touching moments like co-worker who has also been on this journey checking on me and always saying, "You're going to make it. You're a strong woman. Remember that." Touching moments like a senior student volunteering to wrap the bandages on my arm during lymphedema therapy. Touching moments like cards and books from so many people who kept me on their prayer lists. Touching moments like a family friend's son shaving his head for Breast Cancer Awareness month at his school in my honor.

Inspiration from all of the wonderful medical doctors, nurses, techs, and other survivors. Inspiration from the frail old people who were at the offices for chemo and radiation. Inspiration from a former student painting a pink ribbon picture for me and suprising me with it. Inspiration from helping others who have been diagnosed. Blessings abound.

There are so many little joys that we take for granted until they are not there anymore. So, take the time to breathe. Make the time to laugh. Appreciate the ones who love you. Care for others. Give of yourself. Remember that you are not alone. All you have to do is reach out to another survivor, a support group, your friends, your family, and of course, your faith. You can get through this. You are a strong woman.

Chapter Fifteen

In a Nutshell

* Do not diagnose yourself using the Internet.

* Do not get depressed when you are met with bad news . . . . put on your boxing gloves and get ready to fight.

* Do not eat/drink lots of sugar especially between diagnosis and surgery.

* Do not drink water from plastic bottles. NEVER. unless you purchase a bottle that reads, "BPH free", do not drink from plastic. Look it up on the internet. It's complicated, but suffice it to say that more young women are being diagnosed because they keep plastic water bottles in their hands.

* Do not take hormones.

* Choose a surgeon who sees things from your point of view.

* Rest to let your body heal after surgery.

* Plan ahead for your shirt-fillers. Go to a mastectomy products place and get the undershirt and puffs before surgery.
* Buy a wig as soon as you know you have to do chemo.
* Buy cute scarves and hats because the wig situation will get on your nerves after a while. They are hot and itch. And they move around a lot. There is a website I found called Headcovers. com and they have a great variety to choose from. Target and TJ Maxx are also good sources.
* Keep lemonade handy for chemo days. It was the only thing that tasted right.
* If you have to take the "red devil" chemo, take crushed ice and eat it during the treatment to avoid mouth sores.
* Smile at the other patients. Your silent encouragement may be all they get that is positive that day.
* Seek guidance and peace of mind through your faith.

* Talk to other survivors using facebook or websites. Those who have already been down the road you are travelling often provide wonderful insight.

* Stay positive and laugh as much as possible. I believe a good positive outlook is powerful medicine.

Epilogue

There is no real end to this book, because there is no cure for cancer yet. Those of us who are breast cancer survivors, fighters, sisters will always be on this road. We will always be under scrutiny of our own bodies, and we will always be willing to share with others who are embarking on this journey. In the meanwhile, let us all pray that a cure can be found for this and all other cancers. Cancer is such a debilitating disease for the ones who have it, and for the caretakers of those who have it.

Until a cure is found, remember to stay positive, find your inner strength, and don't forget to laugh. All crying will accomplish is stopping up your nose, making your eyes red, and making you sniff a lot. Just remember the phrase I kept telling myself, "This too shall pass." And it will pass.

For the benefit of my English aficionados, I do realize that I have written fragments in places. I was writing as I talk. Who speaks in complete sentences, anyway? So get over yourself. ☺

"Breast wishes" and "ta-ta" for now,

Beverly

Acknowledgements

First, a huge thank you to my friend and colleague, Mrs. Amy Devane for painting the cover of my book. You are so talented and sweet. Thanks a million!

Next, an extra-large thank you to the doctors and staff of Flowers Hospital in Dothan, Alabama. I changed some of the names in the book, but you know who you are!

An "infinity" thank you to my family, friends, and students who have cared for and about me during this journey. JoAnn and Cleveland Bryan, Yvonne Dunlap, Shirley Walker, Steve Still, James and Virginia Ward, Anna Buie, Tiffany, Feng, and John Li, May Huong, Alaina Clark, Ashley Garner, Kacee K. Sims, Kathy Kirkland, Susan Summers, Marsha Johnson, Jim & Jennifer Matheny, Janet Bradley, April Windham, the Sherrers, the prayer warriors from Calvary Baptist Church, Theresa Whitehurst, Martha Jane Sparks, Teresa Wall, Virginia Brookins, Austin Davis, Victor Nieves, Lillie Skeen, Calvin Wilborn, Chris Shaw, my facebook friends, and Ellen Sinclair.

Another gigantic thank you to my colleagues, friends, students, and family members who read and encouraged me to publish this book. Kit Childree, Kelly Dawson, Teresa Wall, Patty Adams, Jane Peterman, Sherrie Salem, Kacee Sims, Yvonne Dunlap, JoAnn and Cleveland Bryan, Steve Still, Ellen Sinclair, Anna Buie, Susan Summers, the Sophomore class of 2013 at NHS, Marsha Rosener, and Chase White.

Finally, a sweet goodbye for now to our friend Jane Brown who left us to be with God in February of this year.